SCIENCE EXPLORER JUNIOR

Think Like a Scientist in the Kitchen

by Matt Mullins

CHERRY LAKE PUBLISHING · ANN ARBOR, MICHIGAN

Published in the United States of America by Cherry Lake Publishing
Ann Arbor, Michigan
www.cherrylakepublishing.com

Content Editor: Robert Wolffe, EdD, Professor of Teacher Education,
Bradley University, Peoria, Illinois

Design and Illustration: The Design Lab

Photo Credits: Page 8, ©iStockphoto.com/kali9; page 11, ©pzAxe/
Shutterstock, Inc.; page 12, ©Panos Karapanagiotis/Shutterstock, Inc.;
page 17, ©gosphotodesign/Shutterstock, Inc.; page 18, ©iStockphoto.
com/GeorgiosArt; page 19, ©newphotoservice/Shutterstock, Inc.; page
23, ©iStockphoto.com/HultonArchive; page 26, ©Paul Orr/Shutterstock,
Inc.; page 29, ©bikeriderlondon/Shutterstock, Inc.

Library of Congress Cataloging-in-Publication Data
Mullins, Matt.
  Think like a scientist in the kitchen/by Matt Mullins.
     p. cm.—(Science explorer junior)
  Includes bibliographical references and index.
  ISBN-13: 978-1-61080-165-2 (lib. bdg.)
  ISBN-10: 1-61080-165-2 (lib. bdg.)
  1. Science—Experiments—Juvenile literature. 2. Science—
Methodology—Juvenile literature. I. Title. II. Series.
  Q182.3.M85 2012
  507.2′4—dc22   2011006544

Cherry Lake Publishing would like to acknowledge the work
of The Partnership for 21st Century Skills. Please visit
www.21stcenturyskills.org for more information.

Printed in the United States of America
Corporate Graphics Inc.
July 2011
CLFA09

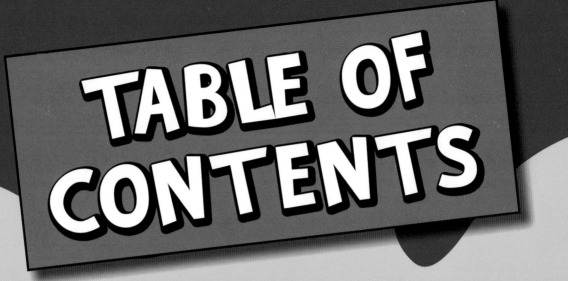

TABLE OF CONTENTS

How Does That Work?

Have you ever wondered about something in your kitchen?

Have you ever looked at something and wondered, "How does that work?" Scientists do that all the time. Even in their kitchens.

Science can help you find out what floats in water and why.

Kitchens are wonderful for cooking, eating, laughing, and learning! You can learn a lot about science in the kitchen. What happens when ice melts? Does everything float? Scientists study **chemistry** and **physics** to find answers to these questions. You can study them yourself, in the kitchen!

You can get your own answers by thinking like a scientist. Go step by step. You may have to repeat some steps as you go.

1. Observe what is going on.
2. Ask a question.
3. Guess the answer. This is called a **hypothesis**.
4. Design an experiment to test your idea.
5. Gather materials to test your idea.
6. Write down what happens.
7. Make a conclusion.

Don't forget paper and a pencil.

Use words and numbers to write down what you've learned. It's okay if an experiment doesn't work. Try changing something, and then do the experiment again.

Write down everything you see and do.

A library is a great place to find science information.

Scientists look for facts before they start an experiment. They use this information as a place to start.

Where can you find information? A library is filled with books, magazines, and science videos that can help you. You can talk to a teacher or a parent. You can visit a museum, too.

You can also find facts on the Internet. Be careful. Not everything on the Internet is the truth. Ask an adult to help you find the best places to look for information.

Adults can help you find the most helpful information.

Water + Heat = Water Cycle!

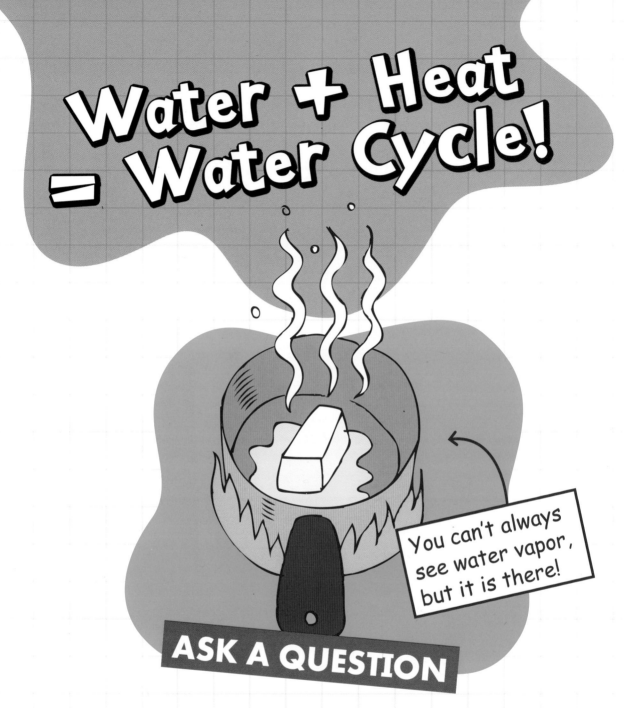

You can't always see water vapor, but it is there!

ASK A QUESTION

Ice melts when you leave it out of the freezer. It turns into water. When you boil water in a pot, it seems to disappear. It turns into water **vapor**.

Do you see the drops of water forming on this teapot's lid?

When you place a cover over hot food, water drops form on the cover as the food cools. What is happening?

A scientist named Aristotle thought about water in nature. He thought that the sun made some water rise into the air as **gas**. Aristotle wrote that the cold caused the water in the air to turn back into liquid and come down. This is the **water cycle**.

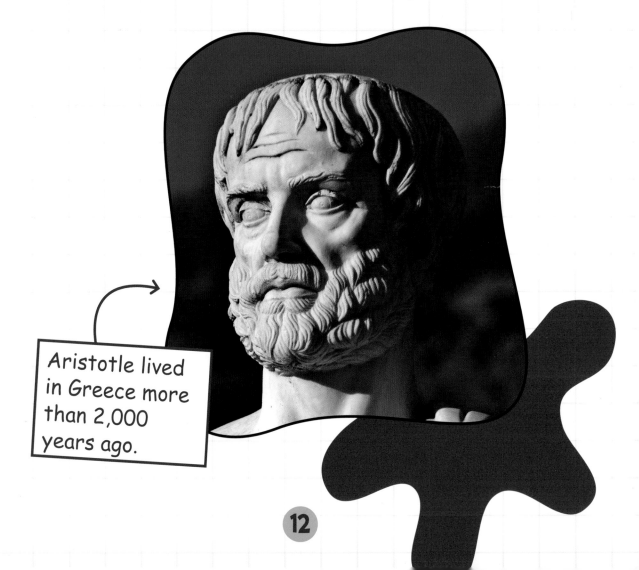

Aristotle lived in Greece more than 2,000 years ago.

When water freezes it becomes ice. When ice melts, it becomes water. When water is heated, it becomes vapor, a gas. Can you make ice into water? Can you make it into vapor? Can you then turn that back into ice or water? Who could you ask?

DO AN EXPERIMENT

Be sure to squeeze the air out of the sandwich bag when you do this activity.

See if you can change water from one form to another. All you need is an adult, a sandwich bag that closes tightly, and a microwave oven. Put two ice cubes in a heavy sandwich bag. Seal it closed with as little air as possible. Now ask the adult to heat it in a microwave.

What happens to the ice as you heat it? It turns to water. Now keep heating it. What happens to the water as you heat it? What happens inside the bag if you cool it down in your refrigerator? If you freeze it? Does the microwave act like the sun in Aristotle's water cycle?

What do you notice about water as it is heated?

Where Did It Go?

If you have ever used powdered drink mix, you have made a solution.

Have you ever mixed a powdered drink? You stir the drink powder into water, and it changes the way the water looks. It changes the way the water tastes, too! Mixing two things like this is called making a **solution**.

What is happening to the powder? Before you mixed it with water, you could see the powder. In the drink, the powder is gone, but the liquid looks different. Where did the powder go? How did the water change color? Who could you talk to about what happened?

Stirring sugar into a cup of coffee creates a solution.

Antoine Lavoisier was a scientist who lived in the 1700s. He thought that when you mix things together, even if they look different, something stays the same. The new mixture weighs the same as the two things did before they were mixed together. Stir salt into water. The weight of the saltwater is equal to the weight of the salt plus the weight of the water.

Antoine Lavoisier studied chemistry in his free time when he was a student.

Workers collect salt that was once mixed with ocean water.

The powder, the water, and the salt all have weight and **mass**. They sometimes change form or appearance, but they don't just go away. Sometimes we can get things back in the form they were before mixing.

Using a clear glass will help you see what is going on in this experiment.

You can explore solutions in the kitchen. All you need is an adult, some water, some salt, and a microwave. Fill a glass about one-fourth full with water. Add 2 teaspoons of salt. Stir until you can't see the salt anymore. Now taste a tiny bit of the mix. It is okay to taste because we know what we added. How does it taste? Do you think the salt is still in the water?

See if you can get the salt out. Pour the salt water into a bowl that can be used in a microwave oven. Then ask an adult helper to heat the salt water in the microwave. Heat it until all the water has turned to steam and gone away. What is left in the bowl? Where did it come from?

What do you see at the bottom of the bowl?

Melt It!

An egg is more dense than a marshmallow.

ASK A QUESTION

Have you noticed that not everything weighs the same? An apple and an orange that are the same size don't usually weigh the same amount. Three marshmallows in your hand take up more space than an egg, but they don't weigh as much. They don't have the same **density**.

Density is something's weight in a certain amount of space. It is a measure of how closely the material in an object is packed together. For example, an egg is more dense than an egg-shaped marshmallow.

A well-known story says that a long time ago, a scientist named Archimedes had a problem. Archimedes solved his problem with his knowledge of density.

Archimedes was a mathematician and scientist who lived in ancient Greece.

Archimedes had to find out if a king's crown was really pure gold. The king wondered if a cheaper, less dense metal had been used to make the crown instead of some of his gold. Archimedes couldn't damage the crown to figure it out! But he knew that a crown of mixed metals would be less dense than a gold crown.

Gold is a very dense metal.

Archimedes got a piece of gold that weighed exactly the same as the crown. He dunked the crown in a container filled to the top with water. He measured how much water came out. Then he refilled the container. He dunked the gold and measured again. The real gold made more water come out of the container. They pushed out different amounts. The crown was not pure gold!

This cereal floats in milk because the cereal is less dense than the milk.

What Archimedes saw was that these two things that weighed the same took up different amounts of space. The dense gold took up less space than the not-quite-pure-gold crown. What things in the kitchen do you see that have different densities?

Gather two glass measuring cups, 4 ounces of baking chocolate, and 4 ounces (1 stick) of butter. Ask an adult to melt the butter in one cup in the microwave. Then melt the chocolate in the other cup. Which cup looks more full? Is that the more dense or less dense material? What can you conclude about the density of butter and chocolate?

Gather everything you need before starting this experiment.

Your Big Idea! Does It Float?

Archimedes worked with his ideas about how things float. Something more dense than water won't float in water. Something less dense than water floats nicely!

Do you like gelatin desserts? You can use them to do an experiment with **buoyancy** and density. Ask an adult to help you make some gelatin in a bowl. Cool it in the refrigerator for 30 minutes. It should have started to set but still be jiggly.

Gather some grapes and some pieces of bananas or apples about the same size as the grapes. Place them on top of the gelatin. Return the gelatin to the refrigerator. Wait at least 4 hours. Then look at your gelatin. What happened to the fruit you put in? Did some stay on top of the gelatin? Did some sink in? What can you conclude about the density of the fruit and the gelatin?

Look around your kitchen. What other questions do you have? Keep thinking like a scientist and try to find the answers!

Write down some more kitchen questions and start experimenting to find the answers!

GLOSSARY

buoyancy (BOI-uhn-see) the ability of something to float

chemistry (KEM-i-stree) the study of substances, what they are made of, and how they react with other substances

conclusion (kuhn-KLOO-zhuhn) the answer or result of an experiment

density (DEN-si-tee) the amount of something in a certain space

experiment (ik-SPER-uh-ment) a test of your idea

gas (GAS) matter that fills whatever container you put it in

hypothesis (hye-PAH-thi-sis) a guess

mass (MAS) the stuff in things that gives it weight

physics (FIZ-iks) the science of matter and energy

solution (suh-LOO-shuhn) a mixture made of something that has been dissolved in a liquid

vapor (VAY-pur) gas formed from something that is usually liquid or solid at normal temperatures

water cycle (WAW-tur SYE-kuhl) the natural cycle of ice melt, pooling, evaporation, and rain, snow, hail, or sleet

FOR MORE INFORMATION

BOOKS

Bardhan-Quallen, Sudipta. *Kitchen Science Experiments: How Does Your Mold Garden Grow?* New York: Sterling Publishing Company, 2010.

Becker, Helaine, and Claudia Dávila (illustrator). *Science on the Loose: Amazing Activities and Science Facts You'll Never Believe.* Toronto: Maple Tree Press, 2008.

Mullins, Matt. *Super Cool Science Experiments: States of Matter.* Ann Arbor, MI: Cherry Lake Publishing, 2010.

WEB SITES

PBS: ZoomSci—Water

pbskids.org/zoom/activities/sci/#water

Visit this site to find more science activities to try.

Rader's Physics4Kids.com

www.physics4kids.com/

Learn more about basic physics at this site.

INDEX

ABOUT THE AUTHOR

Matt Mullins holds a master's degree in the history of science. Matt lives in Madison, Wisconsin, with his son. Formerly a journalist, Matt writes about science, technology, and other topics, and writes and directs short films.